chromgelb 0002

A robot jogging, a politician traveling abroad, a woman in the mirror of her social media account: In his poems, Andreas Korte addresses a contemporary reality that has become almost omnipresent in recent years. It is a world in which the private becomes political, the boundaries between virtuality and reality become blurred, and technology can reveal both its utopian potential or its dark side at any moment.
This volume brings together various series of poems from the last two years that examine the linguistic and visual phenomena from which we naturally construct our concept of the world. Scenes from film, the Internet and computer games make their appearance, as well as works of art from past centuries, travel memories, and political snapshots.

Using an extremely direct and unadorned language, Andreas Korte takes a look at our time in a way that is as surgical as it is poetic.

Andreas Korte, born 1969 in Augsburg, lives and works in Berlin. All poems in this book were written between 2018 und 2020.

First edition 2021, copyright chromgelb, Berlin

Cover photo & design: Andreas Korte

Herstellung und Verlag: BoD – Books on Demand, Norderstedt
ISBN: 9783755708230

Andreas Korte

I Walked Through a Building the Size of a City

poems

I

Start-up

For a long time he wanted
to launch a start-up,
just like people in Berlin
or San Francisco.

On various Internet forums
he carefully informed himself
about capital requirements
and business plans.

The civil war forced him to flee
and he lived for a while
with relatives in Ghana,
but his idea stuck with him.

Three years later he returned
to Mogadishu,
with some savings
and the will to make it.

It became very hot
quite early that day,
and like every morning he
opened the door to his shop.

To Peter Higgs

SUPERSYMMETRY: the jacket carefully folded,
placed over a chair, designed by Marcel Breuer,
tubular steel combined with leather,
modern, comfortable and transparent.

SUSY MODEL: the left pocket of his deep blue shirt
was very practical. He always used it for
a pencil and a black ballpoint pen.
The books on the shelf next to his desk
also had deep blue covers.

SUPERSPIN: he had read his emails at home in the
morning, even though he typically refused to do so.
For breakfast a slice of bread with honey
and a cup of coffee without sugar.

SUPERPARTNER: his own theory
often seemed unlikely to him,
but it was useful as a hypothesis
and carried him through the days.

STANDARD MODEL: the view of the streets of Edinburgh,
business as usual. Cars driving to and from the city center
towards the periphery.
A pedestrian on his way.

A Building the Size of a City

I was waiting at
a traffic light.
Endless red.
Neither a pedestrian
nor a car to see.

I sat in an Italian
restaurant and waited.
No waiter,
no olive oil,
no coffee.

I walked through a building
the size of a city,
between countless concrete pillars
of hexagonal layout.
For a long time now,
no production of ammunition.

Dickinsonia

She had swum
quite far, unusually far,
even by her standards.

Floating between countless
layers of water,
feeling the moment of
transition from warmer
to colder regions.

The gentle wave-like movements
of her transparent body,
which she had perfected over the years,
felt a little less easy today.

She dived deep down,
nestled against a stone,
to rest for a while and
to enjoy the darkness.

Hard to say how much
time had passed,
but she knew she never wanted
to leave this place again.

To Joseph Brodsky

Reddish shimmers
of afternoon light
in a bathtub.
A foil has been attached
to the window,
completely reinterpreting the sun.
A few black and white photos
swim just below the
water's surface.

The wooden floor tells stories
as you walk over it.
The walls are covered with stucco elements
that herald the victory of socialism.

But more than anything the space
proudly presents 32 types of mold,
each more gorgeous than the last,
living together in perfect harmony,
joyfully welcoming the breath and sweat
of new visitors.

Triangles and Rhombuses

First order geometries
for a new kind of people,
the people of the future.

Crossing diagonals connect to
triangles and rhombuses
of different shades.

Where they meet walls
they morph into stucco and wallpaper,
the craze at the time.

The combination of Rococo and
Modernism culminates in
a white armchair for statesmen.

The ladies have their own chamber,
full of portraits, and
a bathroom in purple.

Che Guevara parading outside,
giving friendly greeting,
waving his right hand.

The Barcelona Pavilion

Seven fragments of an orange
Seven fragments of an orange peel
next to a bench
next to a bench in the park
in front of the Barcelona pavilion
in front of the German pavilion
for the 1929 World Exhibition in Barcelona
in front of the pavilion of the Weimar Republic
for the 1929 World Exhibition in Barcelona
in front of the reconstruction
of the German pavilion
for the 1929 World Exhibition in Barcelona,
designed by Mies van der Rohe
designed by Ludwig Mies van der Rohe
designed by Ludwig Mies van der Rohe
and Lilly Reich
With a sculpture by the German artist
Georg Kolbe
With a sculpture by the German artist
Georg Kolbe called „Morning"
Seven fragments of an orange peel
and a piece of aluminium foil

#NoFilter

Perfect lipstick, glowing red.
Tight around the neck:
pearls in three rows.
The eyeliner was particularly
successful today.

Taking some quick selfies:
#NoFilter.
All sides, the left
was always the best.

Love songs, party songs,
he couldn't remember
the lyrics anymore,
but it didn't matter.

It was surprisingly cold on deck.
His whole body started trembling.
The wind hit him like a slap in the face.

Heroes' Square

The hotel is located in a residential area.
Parking offenders are
threatened with a beating.
In a lobby, the business cards
of massage parlors.

The military parade at Heroes' Square,
perfectly organized.
Adjacent an empty embassy,
windows barricaded.
The infinite spaces of a museum,
fiercely contested for decades.

In a restaurant a Yiddish orchestra
is playing a song of lost love.
Waiters with white shirts and bow ties
lift the silver domes of the plates,
just like on the Titanic:
One last meal before sinking.

Dark facades at the front of dark buildings.
The basement bar is full of people
who are no longer needed.
A new era is about to dawn,
and all that remains are memories.

II

Atlas Running

Finally some running.
Summer has long been over.
It is winter.
No more leaves,
just naked trees,
but I like this season.

I'm not running too fast
but also not too slow,
just right.
Its hardly a strain,
my battery has improved
quite a lot recently.

Entering a park,
crossing a meadow.
Good for my joints,
sometimes a little stiff.
I can hear my legs.
My developers need to do
some work on this.

A nice family home some distance away,
two floors, bright facade,
with a dark gray roof.
Maybe the family is
just having lunch.

Passing a bench.
But I don't want to sit right now,
I'm in good shape.
Finally I see a tree
lying in front of me.
This is difficult.

I stand a little distance
in front of it,
then I jump
with both legs,
to land safely again
behind the trunk.

Mountain Tour

What color is snow at night?
The flakes fall threateningly
when you raise your flashlight for a second.

One step follows the other,
pants are all soaked,
you can hardly feel your socks.

The stories you tell
aren't funny anymore,
maybe they never were.

Who ever walked that path
before us forgot to leave his marker.
Our only option is to walk straight ahead.

The mountain itself
can only give us a weary smile:
There are just more important things to do.

Romeo of Rimini

His body had been transformed by the sun,
deep brown and leathery.
His hair was curly as usual.
Recently he stopped dyeing it.

A little wider open than necessary:
the white shirt. He proudly wore
a chain with a medallion,
memories of a distant time.

Driving a young woman in his
small Fiat to the viewpoint
he liked so much,
and which he could rely on.

Her body was extremely bright,
which briefly dazzled him.
He liked her smooth blonde hair,
even though what she was saying
was barely understandable.

When he leaned towards her,
the gearshift jabbed him
and he felt an unpleasant
sting in his rib.

Chopin

Pumpernickel instead of cornflakes today,
a start full of promises:
Westphalian reliability
instead of New York efficiency.

Projects are getting bigger.
A light bulb becomes the center
of the universe, a wedding dress
is declared a masterpiece.

For such a day
there's only one appropriate ending:
Frédéric Chopin's Waltz in D-flat Major,
played a little too fast.

Red Roses

The first ray of sunshine in February.
Icy cold at the foot of a high-rise building,
waiting for me twisted on the docks.
Young people drinking beers
under gas heaters in sidewalk cafes.
Next to a museum
a car bomb explodes.

Each morning a TV station broadcasts
Red Roses: An endless love story,
catastrophically going around in circles.
Why does the main character
want to work abroad,
now that her boyfriend
finally wants to marry her?
They could run the hotel
of his father together,
but a dark secret is floating
like a toxic cloud above everything.

In the evening we meet for
a virtual moose hunt,
inside a deep forest.
That rifle feels good,
only the shoulder hurts
a little when shooting.

Then darkness again.

Shrubs

Shrubs, multileaved,
captured by the general start-up mentality,
spread out on metal grids
with aggressive reproductive strategies,
ready to flood the market
with glistening yellow seeds,
fuelled by venture capital,
limited only temporarily
by three stones,
left by the previous owner,
who, bankrupted long ago,
had moved to the outskirts.

We should quickly launch the app
and thus attract up to 30% more
insects, bees and dragonflies,
who perfectly bring
their social skills

and really deliver.

Day of Glass

It's a day when
everything is reflected:
clouds, the blue of the sky,
mountains, the water itself,
air and
time,

which is standing still today,
as I hold my breath
and the light
with its cutting brightness
dazzles me and leaves me speechless.

On this day,
when clouds turn to ice
and fall from the sky,
you're standing naked in front of me
in the water and don't move.

(Erich Heckel, *Day of Glass*, 1913)

Science Fiction

A man enters a bookstore
specializing in science fiction.
He wears multifunctional clothing,
carrying a grey backpack,
as if he were on his way to an
Antarctic expedition.

He asks a shop assistant
whether a particular author has already
published his second book.
She quickly searches
the Internet and denies it,
whereupon he leaves
the store again,
disappointed.

The End of the 20th Century

I can hardly remember
the end of the 20th century.

Probably a dinner with friends.
Maybe we had risotto with white wine.
Then a walk to the Rhine,
to see the fireworks,
way too much cold champagne,
then way too late to bed.
Next morning
watching ski jumping on TV
with a headache.

I remember vividly
the end of the 20th century.

Basalt stones, lots of them,
with a cut out and
reinstalled funnel,
like a technical device
for unknown applications.
A carefully prepared debris field
from bleak remains
of past years beliefs.

(Joseph Beuys, *The End of the 20th Century*, 1982)

III

Autumn in Berlin

Two palm trees bowing in the rain
and a light brown fern posing silently in the foreground.
The water in the pond hardly seems to move.
In the background two men sing in a choir.

To my left sits a tax consultant.
His young client is a violinist.
A Chinese artist meets her father.
They're talking about Beijing, where it's even greyer.

They talk about her creative projects
and about how strange Berlin sometimes appears.
Her new paintings are all about insects;
they represent longing, she finally states.

They represent love, they represent life.
That was a bit too much for me.
So I pay and walk out into the rain,
where fighting dogs greet and bark playfully.

Winter Approaching

Seven ultimate rules
to prevent complete bleeding out.
It's about setting a strategic orientation
in light of a substantial crisis.

- don't confuse things
- whether one is good or not is up to others to decide
- competition of ideas
- considering several possibilities
- feelings are generally understandable
- conflict has been brewing for years
- the situation is slipping away

A gentleman feels winter approaching.

The Reputation of the Artist

There's nothing to be ashamed of:
pop music and a wild life.
Industry has won,
the artist's reputation is ruined.

How is a work of art created?
Lord have mercy.
Bad reviews are painful,
but this torture is unnecessary.

Our relationship is intact,
but only at the surface.
The only thing that works:
open conflict.

The government wants this
whole thing to continue.
But the truth about today
is being circumnavigated elegantly.

To Gilles Deleuze

A grey book with white letters,
unusual format,
heavy in my hand.
The first pages were opened often,
you can feel the folding.
On page one, several words underscored,
notes with a pencil,
helpless explanations of terms,
that remain impenetrable.
But I learned to distinguish
persevere from *perversion*
and that lingered for a long time.

An audio file,
the first hour of a lecture.
A voice in a Swiss German dialect
tells a story about trees
standing in a forest,
all of them looking similar to each other.
Then another story about
people talking in a pub.

A lecture in a deep voice
about the dreams of a young woman,
with a warning not to get lost in them.
A purple sweater
and long fingernails,
pointing in the air at
the unrecognized.

Shy laughter from the audience.

Death on Honeymoon

A man kills his wife on their honeymoon.
After a tour on a catamaran
he reports her missing and
later entangles himself in contradictions.

First polling stations close in the US,
while the world is waiting anxiously for the results.
The election turns into a vote on
the President's policy.

Potential candidates for German Chancellor
take a stand and
present themselves
by praising their individual strengths.

In Mexico City, about four thousand refugees from
Central America are gathering on their way to the US.
It's another thousand miles to Texas,
and two thousand nine hundred to California.

To Steph

You've been untraceable for several days.
Friends and neighbors were looking for you.
A flyer showed an older photo,
your face slightly
leaning to the left, smiling,
your height, your weight,
red jacket, jeans and snow boots.

Stones shimmering under the water's surface.
The sky was suddenly clear and blue,
after a few cloudy days.
The bare bushes on the riverbank
occupied by frost.
Some more snow
on loamy ground.

Four men pulled you out of the
freezing cold river in a plastic wrap.
Naked, your head smashed,
bruises all over your body
and dried blood.
Strangulation marks on your neck,
fractured bones.
The men looked to the side in shock,
their silence condensed
to white mist.

The Return

I returned at night
in my boat.
The water was completely calm
and the sky full of stars.

It was actually forbidden,
I was aware of that,
but I could calculate the risk
pretty accurately.

I rowed carefully to
to be as quiet as possible.
My boat was small and
I just had a few presents.

Carefully going ashore,
nobody to see.
Just the moon,
shining over the palms.

I took my bag,
looked around in all directions,
and then walked
along the beach, full of joy.

Petri Dish

A flat, circular petri dish,
home to hundreds of brains.
Floating in a slightly salty
nutrient solution.

Brightness,
darkness,
periodically steps
across the room.
The temperature is regular.

Since there's nothing else to do,
and everyday life in the laboratory
is mentally underchallenging,
the brains get lost in
daydreams and utopian visions.

A journey to the sea,
the life of a rock star,
driving along a coastal road
with a convertible
in the south of France,
lying in the sun by the pool,
a drink in the hand.

Ceaseless mumbling.
Neighbours are disturbing,
too little space.
Neon light is reflected brightly
in the glass lid.

To Boris Vian

The film has already been running for 20 minutes.
There was hardly anything left of his novel,
almost unrecognizable.
The characters full of clichés
and who actually cast
this lead actor?

The score was completely different
than discussed.
Way too many strings,
no atmosphere at all.

Enough is enough, he thought,
I'm not gonna take it anymore.
During a quiet moment
he jumped up,
to vent his anger,
and yelled loudly into the audience
how much he hated the movie.

A stabbing pain
drove into his chest
and he blacked out.
He saw the questioning look
of his companion.
While falling he tried
to hold on to a seat.

Long Loop

Entrance to a parking garage.
I'm watching a children's program
on the monitor in front of me
in which elephants are fighting over a balloon.
Gently we glide down one floor.

The driver gives the signal to get out.
A quick push on his key,
two short beeps as confirmation
signal the closing of the car.

Running behind a suit-wearer for a long time,
tattoos on his arms
hidden under a shirt.
A flip phone rings.

Concrete pipe system.
At the end of each passage there is a map
that we study for a long time.
Then moving on, with no end in sight.

Finally an elevator door opens,
we are welcomed by cool air
and soft music, a long loop,
to the fiftieth floor.

The view over a complex organism
of high-rise buildings that
continuously reproduce themselves,
until our eyes can no longer focus.

IV

A Small German Town

Two beds, gently floating
through a room.

In a bar the Carpenters sing
a song about the top of the world.

A long walk through vineyards,
a view of a small German town.

Red traffic light falling through
white curtains at night.

Berlin 1

Blue fitted sheet
on someone else's futon.

Dark brown cupboard,
contents unknown.

Black shoes,
very close to each other.

Plaid curtain,
going well with my shirt.

Berlin 2

French breakfast:
two croissants with jam.

The technological revolution
for curve enthusiasts.

Cappuccino, Caipirinha,
Clubmate, Caprisonne.

Being smart, being up to date,
everything integrated.

Berlin 3

A man in a sleeping bag
concentrates on examining
his timeline.

A waitress
in a Thai restaurant
has a new job.

A pensioner
is in search of
Potsdamer Platz.

A woman
in batik trousers
follows her boyfriend.

Berlin 4

Orange light,
orange trash cans:
urban still life in late summer.

A grey wheeled suitcase.
The owner is staying
just a few days.

A white Maserati
is finding its way
through Prenzlauer Berg.

Red drinks on the next table.
Various projects
in different cities.

Spray

One day,
brighter than the sun itself,
I'm lying on thousands of rocks
in a bay.

The water clear as glass,
the air vibrant from heat,
next to me a young woman
with white skin in a yellow bikini.

Some distance away, a few swimmers.
A little further away a boat.
Hardly any voices to hear,
just the sound of the sea.

I'm trying to read a book:
Boris Vian's "L`Écume des Jours",
but the light is reflected mercilessly
by the pages.
I close my eyes again
and hear spray
gently gliding over stones.

Ishtar

Seven men in white coats,
hair combed back tightly.

A sea of shards, dust and stones,
spread out on long tables.

Here are two fragments that fit together,
or maybe not.

Remnants of characters, the shimmering
a glaze in blue and gold.

Two eyes could form the face
of a warrior or a deity.

Three leaves of a flower,
decorating a lion.

First Dream

Right before my plane leaves for Buenos Aires,
I'm taking a quick look
around an art supply store.

I'm searching for something,
but can't find it. Endless rows
of shelves with brushes, paints and pens.

When four men enter the shop,
all wearing trench coats and hats,
I can immediately feel they came for me.

The men discover me,
pull revolvers out of their pockets
and shoot like crazy.

I hide behind a rack of stretchers.
To my left another customer sinks
to the ground, hit by a bullet.

Blood pours out of his mouth,
flowing onto a white canvas beside him,
forming a long red line.

I run out of the store and I see the plane,
which is located on the roof of a high-rise building.
I climb into the cabin and the pilots take off.

Through a side window I notice
the four men are approaching; panic grows in me,
but the propellers start to move and accelerate.

At the edge of the skyscraper we take off,
but fall forward and steeply into a grove,
when the canvas with the red line
comes to my mind again.

Suddenly I know how I would have finished the painting.

Everything is OK in USA

A day in April.

I`m walking towards the center.
The sky seems unnaturally high.
Light blue, a bit of snow
next to the road.

A police car stops next to me.
The cop slowly rolls down the window
and asks
if everything is OK.

I take down the headphones
of a Walkman
and reply:
„Everything is OK."

The cop nods at me,
closes the window
and moves on
to another mission.

To Rex Tillerson

Your flight was delayed in Nairobi.
On the landing field you almost lost your breath.
The heat was like an impenetrable wall.

Finally in your limousine, fortunately with air conditioning.
You reclined, dazed, in black leather,
undoing one more button of your shirt.

Gliding through dark streets of a strange city,
orange lights in front of hermetic architecture,
strange silhouettes on their way into the night.

The hotel is part of the same chain as in the city before.
The lobby looks familiar to you,
abstract paintings in silver frames.

Later in a vest on the bed, sweat on
the gray hair of your arms. The fan circulates
menacingly as the phone next to you rings.

V

Swaying

Swaying compartment:
A woman in a yellow dress
can't hold on.

Swaying tree tops:
A man carries
a blue raincoat.

A red hammer
kindly offers his assistance
to smash windows.

Cosmic Answers

A million times stronger
than the supercollider.

Tiny life, organic,
on the cutting edge of time.

Colour-coded speeds
steadily increasing.

All the stem cells of Europe have
sufficient space on a chip.

The size of a fingernail
becomes industrially viable.

Many years searching
for cosmic answers.

Silver

Extremely relaxed,
sitting in an office chair.
Hands folded, shoes polished,
the suit is immaculate.

On the table a modernist
sculpture in the form of an arch.
A lamp with a gently curved
neck in silver.

The opened laptop also in silver,
in sleep mode for a long time now.
Leaning against the wall:
a large monochrome painting.

To Rudi Dutschke

A summer evening in Berlin.
Warm light in the streets.
Two photos at a bus stop.

A man with an energetic chin.
A man with a sharp eye.
A man with a fashionable turtleneck sweater.

The photos in black and white,
which means:
Whatever is depicted
is long gone.

The days when anything was possible,
and nothing like before. When generations
faced each other and things were said,
that you didn't dare to say.

What remained was a shoe in the street,
a dark stain on the asphalt
and a white, elegantly curved chalk line,
portrait of a man and his time.

Call of Gravity

A wonderful jump.
Arms out to the side,
one knee drawn up,
the head with a confident look
straight forward.

You stand still
in the air and float,
the sky behind you
full of clouds.

Time is frozen,
for one moment.
Then gravity starts
calling you.

Being pulled down,
your posture remains perfect
as you fall several levels
into a stretched-out net.

The team will take care of you immediately.
All joints are moving,
the hydraulics are undamaged,
but the software could use an update.

A Boy

The skeleton of a boy.
Carefully laid out
on black cloth.

He died
at the age of
seven and a half years.

The volume of his brain was
eighty-seven percent
of an adult brain.

Some bones are missing:
lower legs, feet,
right arm, both hands.

He was a Neanderthal.
His remains were found
in a cave in Spain.

Hello Sophia

Hello Sophia,
good to see you.
Your first steps are impressive.
Gently fumbling,
at the same time confident.
You're waving to me
with slightly stiff arms.

Hello, Sophia,
I hope you're okay.
You seem skeptical
regarding cryptocurrencies
and unfortunately you want to
kill all humans,
but I think that's
only temporary.

Hello, Sophia,
let's meet again
sometime soon.
You will have changed:
maybe a new hairstyle,
new clothes,
and new understanding
for me and my kind.

My Autonomous Car

I wake up. The push-ups feel
a little harder than they used to, but that's okay.

Taking a quick shower, drying off, brushing my teeth.
Unfortunately there's not enough time for breakfast again.

Starting the app to call the car. It will be here in three minutes.
Checking Instagram, a few likes, a new follower.

I'm stepping into the street, the car is approaching
from the right. The door opens, I get in.

The white leatherette seats are nice and soft.
The steering wheel is missed only on rare occasions.

I use the ride to stream a series,
to relax, work, read a book.

Then I'll pick up the kids. They live with their mother.
Rushing to school, then to work.

A lot of stress. Luckily the car picks up
the flowers I will later need for my date.

Four Men of Today

You're sitting in an open denim shirt
on a stool working on your Vespa
in a relaxed manner.
The door to the garage is open behind you.
The house is clinkered,
like so many houses in the Rhineland.
Air pressure checked,
tires changed,
engine repaired,
all without any effort.

You're sitting in the kitchen reading the paper.
The laptop is opened on the table,
in front of you a croissant with some jam.
It's Saturday morning.
You start the weekend slowly,
but it's important for you to be informed.

You're sitting in the open trunk of your SUV.
A dog next to you, well groomed,
with golden-brown fur.
The parking lot of a local recreation area.
It is spring.

In the evening you play some
basketball with your friends.
The ball moves easily between
your left and right hands.
Behind a fence there is a last bus
in front of the yellow facades
of old buildings.

Einstein

Einstein wearing a suit,
a glass in his hand.

Loosely engaged in conversation
with sculptor Maillol.

An art dealer briefly looks
at his pocket watch.

All of them are surmounted by
an elegant lady with short hair.

The Sky Disk

It came as a complete surprise to him.
The blade had penetrated deep into his chest
from the front and left a notch in his spine.
He wanted to scream as loud as he could,
but all you could hear was just a quiet groan.

He had owned the sky disk for years,
it was his most important treasure.
A symbol of his intelligence and open-mindedness.
At important dinners he had
sometimes presented it to his guests,
and proudly talked of the latest discoveries
in the field of astronomy.

A few years later, he had the disk reworked.
An expert came and brought a drawing
of current observations.
It was the goldsmith's job to work out the design
with a few drops of liquid gold.

He looked at the new disk for a long time.
Some more symbols had been added
and he wondered where the stars would take him.

A second stab, professionally done, gladiator style.
From the upper left, past the clavicle,
through major veins. Blood rushed through his
upper body like glowing lava.

In the Yellow Light of a Club

Walking in the evening
between nameless buildings.
The red sky rests gently
on my skin.

I'm meeting two others,
who I don't know and who
don't have anything to say to me.

We just quickly nod at each other,
in the yellow light of a club,
whose members we would like to be.

Then we move on.
We'll ask no questions
and I'll slightly move
the fingers of my right hand.

(Helmut Middendorf, *Cityfeeling*, 1982)

Dangerous Woman

Dangerous woman
in semi-darkness,
illuminated from below.

In the left hand a cigarette.
Right elbow bent, on the belt
a handkerchief with white dots.

Your eyes look
past me; my world appears to be
of little interest to you.

A strange blue light
connects us,
but only I can see it.

Butterfly

A wing of a butterfly
hits me hard,
like a slap in the face,
leaving a strangely shaped,
deep blue mark.

His journey led him
from the banks of the Orinoco
to the temptations of Berlin;
he has every right to demand
some undisturbed rest.

Wings have to be unfolded,
colors and patterns put in order,
legs and antennae stretched
to be in perfect shape
for later appearances.

10 Rules for Authors

1. surprise with the opening

2. avoid new creation

3. do not exaggerate

4. drinks first, then writing

5. expect further losses at any time

6. reveal many salacious details

7. insist on financial compensation

8. work to the limit

9. believe in the ideal scenario

10. always remain hybrid

VI

The Mountain Hut

(To George Michael 1)

A view over the Alps:
snowy slopes, fir forests.
Saas-Fee lies in the valley,
a village in the Swiss canton of Wallis.
We arrive in two SUVs.
I get out of the car
and wave to you.

It's good to see you and the others.
We used to be a close circle of friends,
until the paths of life separated.
I'm accompanied by my new girlfriend
and you're also not single anymore.
In a cable car we go further up the mountain
to a cabin we rented a few weeks earlier.

Everything is prepared nicely.
Designer furniture, but not too modern.
We take care of the room a little bit,
decorate the tree and set the table.

Our eyes meet:
It's the same attraction as before,
but we don't let it show.

Then we run outside
to have a snowball fight.
I stop at a wooden fence
and watch the whole scene from a distance,
with a feeling between
insecurity and melancholy.

In the evening there is an atmospheric dinner.
The highlight is a cake with sparklers,
which a friend of mine is festively
bringing to the table, like a waiter.
The whole room is filled with
conversations and anecdotes
and for a brief moment
our eyes meet again.
I see that your new boyfriend
is wearing the piece of jewelry
I gave to you a year ago
on the lapel of his jacket.
In a quiet moment
I have to think about how you and I
were running through the snow back then,
fell to the ground and kissed.
This piece of jewelry
was a token of my love,
in the shape of a flower,
decorated with diamonds.

I notice that he is carrying
my gift with the flowers facing down,
instead of up, as originally intended.

But while I'm still speculating about
the meaning of this little detail,
a new day has already emerged.
We return in the cable car
back to the snowy valley,
laughing and joking and reminiscing
about the most beautiful moments
of the last few days.

Grove Tower

(to George Michael 2)

A nighttime view over Miami.
The last rays of the evening sun,
sparkling lights on the horizon.

You look ravishing in your short white bathrobe.
I pull you to me. We fall on the bed and kiss.
Through the lowered blinds the light falls in bright pink
on the pleasantly cool bed linen in crimson satin.

In the Watson Island marina, I'm sitting
loosely, leaning against a metal grate.
You are wearing a pink polo shirt over white
tennis shorts and bend over to kiss me.
The tape recorder next to me plays a current pop song,
my left hand moving gently to the rhythm.
We look deep into each other's eyes
and laugh full of happiness.

Another woman gets out of a black limousine
and walks along a road near the beach,
a black leather jacket thrown loosely over her shoulder.
She turns around and looks at me
with flirty eyes.

Together we take a tour on my boat.
The high-cut white swimsuit makes her look very seductive.
She leans against the railing and strokes
her long, slightly wavy hair.
I give her a sign, she sits down next to me
as I put my arm around her.

Then we're in my bedroom,
having passionate sex.
She sits on me, tosses her wet hair back,
I kiss her neck while stroking her breasts.
She pulls me to her and we fall back on the sheets.

I'm still gently asleep when suddenly the door opens
and you're standing in the room, terrified.
With a single glance you have understood the scene
and run away in your blue dress, totally shocked.
I still try to stop you from getting on the plane,
but the pilot has already closed the cabin door.
Through a window you look in my direction for a moment,
only to turn away again.
The seaplane picks up speed and then takes off
towards an unknown destination.

You have pulled off your ring, the ring I once gave you.
I'm standing in a white tennis outfit on the balcony of my
penthouse in the Grove Tower, an apartment building
from 1982. The mixture of Postmodernism and Art Deco
is typical of Miami's architecture. For quite a long time,
I watch the sun go down and the light
slowly changes from rose to pink.

I am aware that I cannot change anything,
and walk from the balcony back to the living room.

VII

Guang Dong

The wrong keyboard arrived
in frustration-free packaging,
Qwertz instead of Qwerty.

I wrote to an older gentleman
in Guang Dong,
a Chinese province
with 106 million inhabitants.

It is bordered on the north
by the Nanling mountains,
on the south by the
South China Sea.

It was raining when he wrote me back.
He was sitting in a restaurant on the coast,
which he had only recently discovered.

After a sip of beer,
he read his answer again briefly
and clicked "Send".

One Day in September

Iran proudly presents
a new warship.
The country feels ready for fresh
conflicts in the Persian Gulf.

The American president promises
an imminent meeting with the North Korean leader.
A date has not yet been set,
but South Korea has welcomed the initiative.

Turkey fights against high inflation
with discount battles.
The fall of the lira has been halted for now,
but the crisis is not over yet.

In Paris, protests against
rising taxes on diesel escalate.
Violent protesters erect
burning barricades made of car tires.

Facades

The building used to belong to the Russian secret service.
You told me that many people had died there.

In the basement, there was a tiled room
with a drain for blood on the back wall.

A sunny day in January.
We had been walking through
the picturesque old town.

Your country was alternately attacked
by Russians or Germans,
but your grandmother said
that the Germans were much more elegant.

I wanted to take a photo of the facade
and took a step forward
for a better view.

Where I had stood just a moment earlier,
a stone the size of a fist, a decorative element,
fell from the roof, bursting in front of me
with a loud bang.

Second Dream

The sun is shining mercilessly.
A brutal cop pulls me
in handcuffs behind him.
He had beaten me up pretty badly;
blood is dripping from my forehead and mouth
and forms a trail on the sand.

He opens the door to a prison,
pushes me in and I fall
to the floor in front of him.
My shoulder hurts like hell.
The cop says something to a woman,
who is sitting behind a desk.
She puts a sheet of paper into
of her typewriter and starts typing.

I seize the opportunity and throw myself on
my tormentor, who is goes down hard.
In his left trouser pocket I find the
keys to the handcuffs and unlock myself.
The woman sits motionless behind her desk,
observing the whole scene calmly.
She continues to write while humming a song.

I pull the unconscious man into another room,
and tie him up in a corner.
The windowless room is furnished
only with a chair and a table.
On the tabletop there is a drill,
which sparks my interest. I look at it
for a long time, letting the drill spin in the air.

I'm carefully drilling a hole in the middle of the table,
bending over and looking with one eye
directly into the black hole.
In the midst of the darkness I recognize
a spot of light slowly approaching.
It gets bigger and bigger,
finally transforming into a view
of an alpine landscape.

Suddenly I lose my grip,
falling completely into the black hole,
only to find myself next to a lake,
surrounded by a vast mountain range.
I happily take a walk
and enjoy the clean air.

Josephine

Josephine is a young woman with black hair,
tied into a braid. Her profile photo shows her
entwined by autumn leaves with the slogan
"I am grateful".

In the only picture she posted,
you can hardly see her. She's standing
near the shore of an artificial lake,
on a summer day somewhere in Texas.

Up to her waist in the water,
she's wearing a green T-shirt
and looks straight ahead into the camera,
without any particular emotion.

The photographer of this scene
is standing on the other side of the lake
and only seems to be
present by accident.

Sad Young Man on a Train

Sad young man on a train.
Whom should he approach?
He turns around, he's had enough,
how will it end for him?

I see him and he sees me,
my eyelid moves down
and up, light again,
but he's already disappeared.

Where space and time are not parallel,
just wiggling their way through the universe,
you can't buy a solution
to escape the black nothingness.

You and I will rush simultaneously
inside the postulate of infinity
through a large orbit
in the direction of a surrogate of progress.

(Marcel Duchamp, *Sad Young Man on a Train*,1911)

The Flynn Effect

The Flynn Effect seems to be reversed lately,
which means that the IQ of humanity
is generally no longer increasing,
but actually shrinking.

I can confirm that.
Recently talking
gets harder and harder,
single words
are barely tangible.

Language in itself
mysterious.
Communication
hardly possible.

Even numbers
are becoming alien
and weird.

I am
also
getting
quickly
tired.

Somewhere in Germany

White frost on bare branches.
A hunter's seat hidden in a spruce forest.
Behind a green noise barrier
a mobile phone antenna provides reception.

Recent snowfall in a colony of allotment gardens.
Mixed forests of nameless trees
limit a wide field, then first buildings,
detached houses with a red pointed roof and garage.

In between some older farmhouses
corrugated zinc sheet silos
with puzzling technical features.
The horizon gets lost in the fog.

Weathered posters on a concrete bridge.
The power lines are frozen.
Another mobile phone antenna
is growing towards the sky in loneliness.

The Churches of Kreuzberg

The churches of Kreuzberg
let the bells ring:
heavy syncopations
on a Sunday morning.
Today it is all about the big picture.

Yesterday, godless debauchery,
dancing ecstasy
and sexual inferno,
colorful costumes
in pulsating rhythms.

All this washed away by the rain.
Leaves fall gently on the remains of
vodka bottles, cups and condoms.
Rather encouraged by this, the pastor takes action
and presses the decisive button,
to set the bells in place.

Or are there still any bell-ringers today,
who live in the attic of churches
and sneeringly swing
on thick ropes?

Luxury, Silence, Lust

Afternoon is almost over.
The sun turns from yellow to blue,
to purple, to red, to black.
Our skin is heated and full of sweat.

A sailboat is lying on the shore.
We came at dawn:
six others and I, searching for the same.
The day was within reach.

We had tea and ate some bread,
in the shade of a cedar tree,
and our bodies met
in seemingly endless light.

When time finally passed,
we're all very aware,
that this moment will end now,
like a yellow cloud that fades away.

(Henri Matisse, *Luxury, Silence, Lust*, 1907)

Anti-Andreas

Anti-Andreas was recently
discovered at Cern in Geneva.
During a series of experiments
protons with unimaginable
speed were brought to collision,
so that a black hole was briefly formed
and Anti-Andreas appeared.

All the things that are possible with me,
are theoretically also possible with him.

Like me he likes to have
a croissant with his coffee
and his fashion sense
could be a bit better.
Anti-Andreas is interested
in contemporary art,
plays chess and tennis,
likes to read thrillers,
has a weakness
for French philosophy
and generally tends
to obsessive behavior.

Basically, we're
avoiding each other
since any encounter
would cause an uncontrollable
energy flash.

Hanna and the Simulated Men

The shoes don't look good.
Black sneakers would be better
and also a different shirt.
Absurd pattern.
Let's choose a beard,
a three-day stubble is best.
Hair combed up.

The thighs are still a bit too wide,
but the jeans look good.
The eyes could be a little bigger,
the other chin fits better.
The nose is actually quite alright.
Keep it like that.

His name is Leon,
he looks like he's in his twenties.
Maybe a college student, business or law.
He's about to move into a house
with three other men,
and four women.

One of them is you.

Bielefeld

Numerous family houses,
idyllically situated at a river.
The chimney of a factory
sends white smoke into the sky.

Office buildings in the style of postmodern
commercial architecture hope for start-ups.
A multiplex cinema shows
"Immenhof - The Adventure of a Summer".

Graffiti wearily dances on brick walls;
the silver varnish of the letters
reflects the sun's rays just as intended.
An expressway on stilts
brutally pushes forward.

Slightly elevated, an architect
has fulfilled his life's dream
and pays homage to early modernism
with a series of white cubes.

Some distance away a
slowly rotating wind turbine
is determined to claim an existence
as a contemporary sculpture.

Just Another Day in January

Scientists from Canada have discovered radio waves
from far beyond our galaxy.
They cannot completely rule out the possibility
that an unknown life form may be the sender.

The American president will not travel to Davos
for the World Economic Summit due to the ongoing wall
dispute. He blames the Democrats. The shutdown
is already on its twentieth day.

A young hacker gained access to the private data of numerous
German politicians and has published it on Twitter.
The twenty-year-old student wanted to expose
the politicians with his act.

A group of four men are on trial in Berlin.
They are accused of having stolen
a one-hundred-kilogram gold coin
from a museum. There is no trace of the loot.

To Peter

It's about five pm.
You're driving your burgundy Mercedes.
Before the last entrance on the right
you stop the car,
get out, open the gate,
and slowly drive into the garage.

You remove the ignition key,
take the attaché case from the passenger seat,
close the car first,
then the gate from inside
and enter our garden through
a small metal door.

It is summer, the terrace door is open.
In the living room the TV set is running
and I'm sitting on the sofa,
eating a slice of toast.

A quick "hello," just a nod, immersed
in the action of a television series, *Bonanza*.

Adam Cartwright angrily left the Ponderosa Ranch
after a fight with his brothers.
A few days later, with no news
the brothers set out to find him, full of sorrow.

You walk along the hall to the wardrobe
to hang your jacket on a hanger
and put your attaché case down.

To Christa

I wanted to ask you something.
When you were dead for a moment,
what did it feel like?

Was it pleasant, like you're becoming very light
and floating; you rise from your body
and then see the world from outside?
Maybe you look at yourself, a team of doctors
standing around you at an operating table,
hectically initiating emergency measures.

Or did you see your life flash before your eyes?
Your childhood and youth during World War II,
your first job as a secretary in Hamburg,
your marriage, the kids, the house,
the garden, summer, heat, winter, trees, clouds,
your children moving out, your parents dying,
the births of your grandchildren,
blue skies, snow, rain, days, nights.

Is it more abstract, with a bright light
that magically attracts you and
promises endless peace and happiness?
Which is only small at first,
then becomes bigger and bigger
and shows the ultimate way out.

Maybe just nothing, no feelings, no thoughts,
complete absence of anything?
The pure nothingness, where past and future
become irrelevant and consciousness dissolves.

IX

Draft for a Series

I
The construction of the machine

II
A random meeting

III
Journey to the end of time

IV
Hiking through a distant mountain region

V
A misunderstanding is cleared up

VI
Loss of innocence

VII
Return to the starting point

VIII
A surprising confession

IX
What was left

X
Epilogue

The Last Days of Mankind

He prepared another cup of tea
and then sat down at his desk.
Aware that this was the end,
he took out a blank piece of paper,
to write some last lines,
even though there was no longer an addressee.

He thought of his childhood and youth
and the little he could remember
from the years
when there still were others.

He hadn't seen anyone for a long time.
The streets were empty and he had
not left his apartment recently.
His back was hurting,
every move was hard for him
and his lungs made strange sounds
when he breathed.

An old song had remained in his head,
nothing special, a simple song he liked.
It seemed like all the other memories
were outshone by it and there were quite a few things
he'd rather not think about anymore.

Tens of thousands of years of human evolution
now culminated in his person.
He laughed for a moment. Not exactly a climax,
but whatever.

Since he couldn't think of anything else,
he wrote the chorus of the song
on the blank piece of paper.

Hero of the Story

The hero of the story,
reborn in the body of a stranger,
beaten up multiple times,
numerous gunshot wounds.

He found himself in an alien world,
which wasn't his,
living among strangers
in a strange century.

Being very popular with women,
spontaneous sex was not a problem,
but never put him in a state
of emotional dependence.

His destiny will be fulfilled in 10 episodes
and I'm starting to feel guilty
because of my lack of attention.
I'm almost afraid he'll go on without me.

Assassins of Athens

A few more steps ahead to the mountain top,
to enjoy a perfect view over the city,
that seems to go on endlessly
and touches the clouds on the horizon.
Protected by a wall in the foreground,
that even the bravest warriors could not overcome,
symbol of our advanced engineering skills.

My ship is entering the bay.
It's a clear day, full of sunshine,
I'm walking calmly through the port,
past merchants offering elaborately decorated pots
and vegetable farmers who, in addition to lettuce
and cucumbers, also sell exotic fruits.

I'm looking at some murals,
showing scenes of everyday life.
The passage of a gate is flanked by
blue flags with the symbol of an owl.
Sculptures in the shape of warriors and thinkers
greet me silently.

In the sculptors' district, where numerous artists
work their enormous stones in parallel,
an eagle spreads its wings.
The artist is just decorating the pedestal.

A temple surrounded by warriors of pure gold.
Marble lions stand in shallow pools of water.
At the end of the path are columns with burning torches.
I sit down on a bench for a moment
and cool my arms in cold water.

Draw

A short tap on the metallic button
and my clock starts running.
Just for a second I look into
the eyes of my opponent.

Two plus two equals four,
four plus four equals eight,
eight plus eight equals sixteen,
sixteen plus sixteen equals thirty-two.

I think back
to previous games,
and the space around me
starts spinning for a moment.

Thirty-two plus thirty-two
equals sixty-four,
sixty-four plus sixty-four
equals one hundred and twenty-eight.

This constellation seems
familiar to me,
and I start dreaming again
of similar games.

One hundred and twenty-eight
plus one hundred and twenty-eight
equals two hundred and fifty-six.
Two hundred and fifty-six
plus two hundred and fifty-six
equals five hundred and twelve.

Suddenly I'm hungry
and annoyed with my shirt,
which I do not like at all,
and the jacket,
which really is a little too tight.

Five hundred and twelve
plus five hundred and twelve
equals one thousand twenty-four.
One thousand twenty-four
plus one thousand twenty-four
equals two thousand forty-eight.

Also, it's too hot in here and I'm swiping
the sweat from my forehead.
The wound next to my eye
starts pulsating
under the sticking plaster.

Two thousand forty-eight
plus two thousand forty-eight
equals four thousand ninety-six.
Four thousand ninety-six
plus four thousand ninety-six
equals eight thousand one hundred ninety-two.

Attempt to Write a German Schlager

An easy and catchy German Schlager
with sentimental and not very demanding lyrics.

Can't be that difficult.

Simple rhyme scheme,
clear song structures.
No wonder 51% of men
and 59% of women
like German Schlager.

Adorno, of course, rejected them completely,
because they only offer a substitute for feelings,
as part of some false self-ideal,
to numb any revolutionary thoughts,
in late capitalist power structures.

The best thing to write about is love,
the feeling of being in love.
But nothing erotic,
that would be over the top.

Or to talk about home,
maybe something in Bavarian dialect,
after decades of trying
to speak only High German.

I'll put that aside for now,
to work on it later.

At Night in Berlin

At night in Berlin,
when the dust cloud of creativity
is slowly sinking and
people become calmer,

two actors are presenting
themselves as a couple in public
for the first time,

a dead cleaning lady
is lying in Tiergarten, her blood
slowly dropping into the humid grass,

an athlete is sitting
alone in his apartment
rubbing a cream
on his aching knee,

a politician is reading
his speech for the next day,
for the very last time.

Porto

When we finally saw the sea
there was no one left.
Laughter had disappeared,
just like shouting, tanning and thirst.
So we spread out our towels,
side by side and closed our eyes.

The beach.
The next morning.
No measure of distance
other than your own exhaustion.

In the evening we sat together
in the last restaurant in town
that was still open,
and heard our forks
scratching over plates.

Darknet

Nothing but darkness in the darknet.

Bitcoin crashed,
arms trading
no longer works,
drugs pile up on the shelves.

Nothing but darkness in the darknet.

No one remembers any passwords,
Porn is just boring
and credit cards are no longer
worth anything.

Nothing but darkness in the darknet.

Songs all sound the same,
the last web pages are being shut down
and message boards are deserted.

Nothing but darkness in the darknet.

Contract killers retrain
and learn some manual craft,
or something with people.

The Apple

On the first day
of my art studies
I was too late.

I was new in town and got on
the wrong subway in the morning.
Finally at the right stop,
in an industrial neighbourhood,
I couldn't find my way
and got lost among strange
factory buildings that
silently stared at me.

When I finally entered the classroom
I walked past tables
where others were already sitting
in front of an apple,
determined to paint it.

I was welcomed fiercely by my professor:
"You're late. You already missed
the decisive hour of the class,
and I'm not sure,
how you're gonna make it up."

He should be right,
I still miss that one hour:
a crucial piece of information
a missing link,
the key of salvation.

Third Dream

There is an Art Biennial in a multi-storey industrial hall.
I walk aimlessly through empty spaces,
but there is no art to be found, just production leftovers
of rusty steel and broken glass.

The floor is covered with a thick layer of dust,
everything seems to have been abandoned for years.
I pick up a piece of steel from the floor, look at it
from all sides and drop it again.
Lonely sound wanders through the rooms.

At the end of a corridor I find a staircase that takes me
to the upper floor, where a group of people are sitting
in a big circle of chairs mumbling incoherently.
A man with a beard looks into my eyes
and points to an empty chair next to him.

As I sit down, the others suddenly fall silent and turn to me.
The bearded man with gives me a yellow tennis ball,
which I'm looking at closely from all sides.
As I put it into the pocket of my jacket,
everyone goes back to their mumbling.
I get up and leave the factory.

Standing on the street again, an Afghan Hound
approaches me. He sits down on the asphalt,
his groomed fur shining in the sun.
I remember the tennis ball, take it out of my jacket
and throw it far down the road. The dog runs wildly after it,
catches it and disappears around the next corner.

Florence

The long years in a man's life.

Tour buses are grouping together to form a ballet.

Clark Gable's doppelganger.

The travel plan of a Japanese tourist.

A football hovers over a treetop.

Bread without salt.

The reddish evening light shining on a hand of marble.

Phosphorus in the water of a lake.

Nightly motorcycles howl at the moon.

An espresso tastes extremely bitter.

Opportunity

We haven't heard from you in months.
The sandstorm became impenetrable.
You worked for us for fifteen years.
It's hard to understand what it means
to be always on your own
for such a long time.

A Sol, which means a day on Mars
lasts 37 min longer than one day on Earth.

In the beginning Spirit was still your companion,
I can imagine
that you didn`t just work,
but also talked about private matters.
Maybe you were friends.
It must have been very sad,
when he failed.

After that just
red dust
and rocks.

Autocorrect until the End of Time

The last few days we were in the air
I had the end of the world and the sun
on the way to the city in the last
months and years in my hand.

I run towards time and desire on the table.
The last three years
facing the end of time and
of the sun.

The last days in the city
I saw a YouTube video,
and it was a very nice evening
and a great success.

I'm running late
and I've expressed myself several times
in the last two hours
and the last three days
in vague terms.

Dark Matter

Considering that the visible world
with sofas, tables and lampshades
equals just 5% of the universe,
it's amazing that anything
even exists at all,

instead of just nothingness.
Existence as a special case,
a brief confusion,
which will soon settle down,
when normal state is reset again.

Three colored tubes: red, yellow, blue.
A pair of headphones,
two round coasters made of cork
and four oranges.

The rest: only dark matter, nameless.
Nobody ever saw it,
no properties,
no smell.

But powerful enough,
to move stars.

Couple

A woman is sitting on the back of a sofa.
She looks really attractive
in her tight jeans and
black high heels.

She feels comfortable in her living room
and the shoes match the pillow
next to her.

A man is leaning against the radiator.
Shortly shaved hair, dark eye circles,
a phone in his right hand.
He's freezing, and he'd like to
call someone.

Yellow Fever

Lying with a sore shoulder,
hoping for salvation
through encoded proteins.

It's how I navigate the jungle cycle,
the smell of a summer in lemon yellow
remaining in my nose.

Slightly feverish from tree to tree.
Short greeting to the primate friend:
The fruit tastes sweeter than usual today.

Chased by hostile vectors,
drawn to the pulse of the city,
I lay down and finally learn to walk upright.

Twilight

If you get mugged,
don't fight back.
Just hand it all over.

Watches, jewelry, wallet,
smartphone, cash card;
money isn't important.

Recently someone got shot
at the university
over an iPhone.

Please come back,
with your head
on your shoulders.

Returning from the breakfast buffet
I find a piece of papaya
in my hair.

My room is decorated
with harmless attempts
at abstract painting.

In this version
of Love Island it`s unclear
what the young people are actually doing.

Also unclear
is whether there are any insects
in this town at all.

Stefan George
is the only German poet
in a bookstore.

"Crepúsculo",
Portuguese for
twilight.

The envelope shows the poet
with piercing look and
dynamic hair.

The mood is dark,
as usual, wrapped
in black fabric.

Memories of a river
I never saw
but have often heard of.

Fingers, which wander across
the steel strings
from bottom to top,

which, even when it seems hopeless,
feel meaning
and truth.

Memories of a river,
that I'll find again,
and will give me a friendly smile.

Young men happily
race through the alleys
on electric scooters

and cheerfully
shout out their
next target,

while I am worn down
like Gustav von Aschenbach
sitting at the Lido, out of breath,

make-up running down
my cheeks,
drawing dark lines.

The lover
with strongly gelled,
combed-back hair.

The woman in a short red dress,
her blonde hair, shoulder-length,
with traces of a past perm.

He takes one step forward,
puts his hand to her cheek
and points his lips as if he would kiss her,

only to turn round surprisingly
and leave the room, because another,
more important project demands his attention.

A family is sitting at the breakfast table.
All white, typical middle class:
father, mother and two children.

It's a Sunday morning.
They sit in the comfortable kitchen and eat
rolls with a German hazelnut cream.

A couple on a balcony,
both white, very attractive,
successful at work as well as in private life.

They enjoy a free Sunday,
each with a roll in their hand,
covered with that same hazelnut cream.

At 3:43 a.m., the inevitable
moment of great awakeness,
in the rhythm of home.

Two bars of four beats each,
in a swing feeling that's
hard to quantify.

Origins in Angola and the Congo,
created in Rio de Janeiro
with numerous variations.

The city allows itself
a moment of peace
and the air conditioning takes over.

A Polish Violinist

A Polish violinist
with a strong reluctance
against all forms of technology
sits in my kitchen
and contemplates the
fall of the occident.

There can be no more
music after Led Zeppelin,
that much is certain for him.
You shouldn`t actually be
listening to music anymore.

One day he rings my doorbell,
comes running up,
borrows my phone
for a quick call,
says „thank you",
turns around
and rushes back down
the stairs again.

Bauhaus Dessau

The coffee mug appears unusually large,
big enough to drown in.

I wash my hands and dry them
in the hot air of a British designer.

There is another visitor in the opposite wing of the building.
We look into each other`s eyes for a moment.

Not easy to take a good photo of a chair,
when it is standing in front of a large window.

Some movies run on monitors that position themselves
in a secret area between the second and third dimensions.

I knock on a grey metal door.
Other doors have bells.

Even careful consideration can not uncover
the layers of sand from the past.

On one desk there is an old typewriter.
A visitor wrote on it: „I remember you".

I Am Not a Robot

I am not a robot.
This shows in my ability to distinguish
images of mountains and hills from
images of streets and parking garages.

They are desert-like areas,
sparse vegetation
under a relentless sun,
probably somewhere in California.

I know these places mostly from movies,
with desperate lead characters,
sweat running down their faces,
trying to escape a mysterious pursuer.

I have that advantage over robots:
The endless hours
I spent watching these movies,
that have made me the man
I am today.

Contents

Some poems were inspired by works of art. Thanks to the artists, as well as to the museums and collections that keep these works alive.

Erich Heckel, *Day of Glass*, 1913, Bayerische Staatsgemäldesammlung
Joseph Beuys, *The End of the 20th Century*, 1982 - Bayerische Staatsgemäldesammlung
Helmut Middendorf, *Cityfeeling*, 1982 - Privatsammlung
Marcel Duchamp, *Sad Young Man on a Train*,1911 - Peggy Guggenheim Collection
Henri Matisse, *Luxury, Silence, Lust*, 1907, Musée d'Orsay

chromgelb 2022